THE POWER OF POSITIVITY

THE POWER OF GRATITUDE

BY ABBY COLICH

BLUE OWL BOOKS

TIPS FOR CAREGIVERS

Social and emotional learning (SEL) helps children manage emotions, create and achieve goals, maintain relationships, learn how to feel empathy, and make good decisions. The SEL approach will help children establish positive habits in communication, cooperation, and decision-making. By incorporating SEL in early reading, children will be better equipped to build confidence and foster positive peer networks.

BEFORE READING

Talk to the reader about what it means to feel grateful. Ask them what they are thankful for.

Discuss: Name something you are grateful for. Why do you think it is important to talk about what you are grateful for?

AFTER READING

Talk to the reader about the different ways they can practice gratitude and the benefits they may experience from doing so.

Discuss: Why is it important to practice gratitude? What is one thing you can do to practice gratitude more often?

SEL GOAL

Children may have a difficult time understanding the benefits of practicing mindfulness. Explain to children that certain actions can trigger reactions in the brain. These reactions can affect how they feel in their mind and body. Practicing forms of mindfulness, such as gratitude, can help them feel good.

TABLE OF CONTENTS

CHAPTER 1
What Is Gratitude? 4

CHAPTER 2
Gratitude Is Good for You 8

CHAPTER 3
How to Practice Gratitude 14

GOALS AND TOOLS
Grow with Goals 22
Try This! 22
Glossary 23
To Learn More 23
Index 24

CHAPTER 1

WHAT IS GRATITUDE?

Gratitude is showing **appreciation** or giving thanks. You probably say "thank you" when someone gives you something. It is polite and good manners. It also helps you feel **grateful**.

Feeling grateful helps you appreciate what you have. Willa's dad made her a cake for her birthday. She feels grateful.

CHAPTER 1 5

Gratitude is something you can **express**. You can write a thank-you note or tell others what you are thankful for.

Gratitude is also something you can practice. When you practice gratitude, you think about what is good around you. You might spend a few minutes a day writing about what you are grateful for.

WHAT CAN YOU BE GRATEFUL FOR?

You can feel grateful for objects, like your home or toys. You can also feel grateful for people, like family members and friends. You can be grateful for **experiences**, like visiting the zoo, too.

CHAPTER 1

CHAPTER 2

GRATITUDE IS GOOD FOR YOU

Julie's brother helps her with homework every day. Julie practices gratitude by saying thank you. Practicing gratitude **benefits** your mind and body. It helps you feel good.

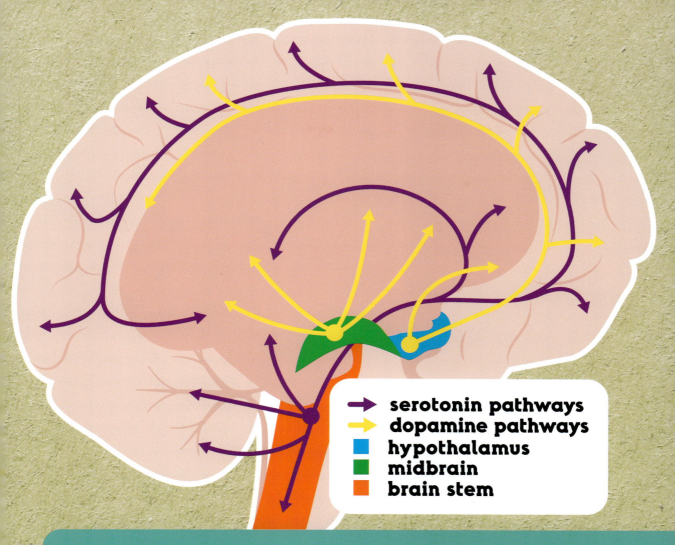

Our brains make **neurotransmitters**. Some are released when we're grateful. Dopamine is one. It is made in the hypothalamus and parts of the midbrain. It makes us feel excited and happy. It also helps us stay focused and motivated. Serotonin is another. It is made in the brain stem. It boosts our mood and helps us sleep better.

CHAPTER 2

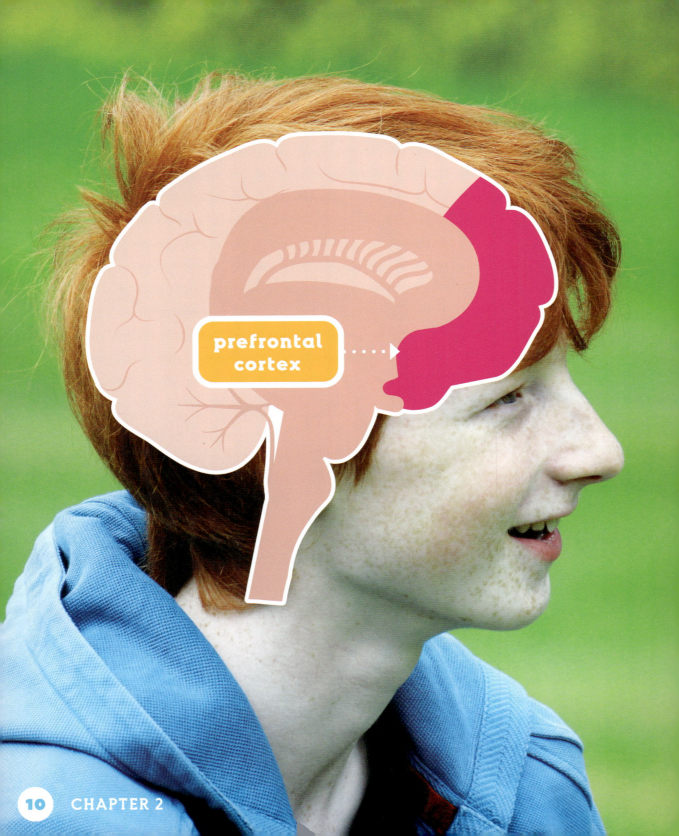

How do we know? Scientists have studied the brains of people who practiced gratitude. Parts of their prefrontal cortex became active. The prefrontal cortex helps us learn, make decisions, and feel **rewarded**. It also helps us feel **empathy**.

GRATITUDE HELPS YOUR BODY

Practicing gratitude can keep you from getting sick as often. It can help you heal faster when you do.

CHAPTER 2

Scientists talked to people who practice gratitude. The people said they felt calmer and less **stressed**. They felt more **optimistic**. They were able to see the good around them.

Raja is stressed about a big test. She thinks about what she is grateful for. She thinks about her friend who helped her study. She feels better.

CHAPTER 3

HOW TO PRACTICE GRATITUDE

We can find time every day to practice gratitude. Colby is thankful for his dog. He shows it by playing with him.

Start by thinking about what makes you happy. Write down one thing each day. Ellie writes in her gratitude journal. She writes about eating her favorite foods with her family.

CHAPTER 3　15

Take time to express your gratitude to others. You might tell your friend, "I'm grateful that you play with me every day." Or you could write a thank-you note to a teacher who helped you.

REMEMBERING GRATITUDE

What is one of your favorite memories? It could be your birthday or the day you got a new pet. What makes this memory so special? Who was there? How could you thank them now? Think about past times you are grateful for. How do you feel?

CHAPTER 2

Meditating is another way to practice gratitude. Sit in a quiet, comfortable place. Close your eyes. Imagine a time you were happy and full of gratitude. Slowly breathe in and out for a few minutes. Do you feel differently than when you started? Meditating can help you stay **mindful** of how you feel and what is good in your life.

Practicing gratitude helps keep our minds and bodies healthy. When you take time to practice gratitude every day, you will feel calmer. You will have more empathy and feel closer to others.

PAY IT FORWARD

Do something kind for another person. Don't expect anything in return. Acts of kindness can help you feel good, just like being grateful.

CHAPTER 3

GOALS AND TOOLS

GROW WITH GOALS

Practicing gratitude has many benefits for both your mind and body.

Goal: Spend a few minutes every day thinking about what you are grateful for. This could be at bedtime. Set a timer for two minutes. Meditate or think about what you are grateful for.

Goal: Express your gratitude. It is never too late to write a thank-you note or tell someone you are grateful for what they do for you.

Goal: Go on a gratitude walk. Take a walk around your home or neighborhood. See how many things you can find that you are grateful for.

TRY THIS!

Create a gratitude box. Decorate a cardboard box and keep it somewhere you will see it often. Every day, write down on a piece of paper something you are grateful for and put it in the box. If you have a bad day, take a piece of paper out of the box and read it.

GLOSSARY

appreciation
The feeling of enjoying or valuing somebody or something.

benefits
Produces good or helpful results or effects or promotes well-being.

empathy
The ability to understand and share the emotions and experiences of others.

experiences
Things a person can do or have happen to them.

express
To show what you feel or think with words, writing, or actions.

grateful
Thankful and appreciative.

meditating
Thinking deeply and quietly.

mindful
A mentality achieved by focusing on the present moment and calmly recognizing and accepting your feelings, thoughts, and sensations.

neurotransmitters
Chemical messengers in the body that send information from one neuron to another.

optimistic
Believing things will turn out well or for the best.

rewarded
Feeling satisfied or encouraged.

stressed
Experiencing mental or emotional strain.

TO LEARN MORE

Finding more information is as easy as 1, 2, 3.

1. Go to www.factsurfer.com
2. Enter "**thepowerofgratitude**" into the search box.
3. Choose your book to see a list of websites.

GOALS AND TOOLS

INDEX

acts of kindness 20
appreciation 4, 5
benefits 8
body 8, 11, 20
brain stem 9
dopamine 9
empathy 11, 20
experiences 6
grateful 4, 5, 6, 9, 12, 16, 20
gratitude journal 15
hypothalamus 9
meditating 19
midbrain 9
mindful 19
neurotransmitters 9
optimistic 12
prefrontal cortex 11
rewarded 11
serotonin 9
stressed 12
thank-you note 6, 16
write 6, 15, 16

Blue Owl Books are published by Jump!, 5357 Penn Avenue South, Minneapolis, MN 55419, www.jumplibrary.com

Copyright © 2024 Jump! International copyright reserved in all countries. No part of this book may be reproduced in any form without written permission from the publisher.

Library of Congress Cataloging-in-Publication Data

Names: Colich, Abby, author.
Title: The power of gratitude / by Abby Colich.
Description: Minneapolis, MN: Jump!, Inc., [2024]
Series: The power of positivity | Includes index.
Audience: Ages 7–10
Identifiers: LCCN 2023029065 (print)
LCCN 2023029066 (ebook)
ISBN 9798889966869 (hardcover)
ISBN 9798889966876 (paperback)
ISBN 9798889966883 (ebook)
Subjects: LCSH: Gratitude—Juvenile literature.
Classification: LCC BF575.G68 C65 2024 (print)
LCC BF575.G68 (ebook)
DDC 179/.9—dc23/eng/20230706
LC record available at https://lccn.loc.gov/2023029065
LC ebook record available at https://lccn.loc.gov/2023029066

Editor: Katie Chanez
Designer: Emma Almgren-Bersie
Content Consultant: Megan Kraemer, MSW, LICSW

Photo Credits: pakww/Shutterstock, cover; FatCamera/iStock, 1; Photoevent/iStock, 3; Dmitry Marchenko/Alamy, 4; Evgeny Atamanenko/Shutterstock, 5; SeventyFour/Shutterstock, 6–7; 88studio/Shutterstock, 8; mtreasure/iStock, 10–11; Backgroundy/Shutterstock, 12–13; Erickson Stock/Alamy, 14; StockImageFactory.com/Shutterstock, 15; YakobchukOlena/iStock, 16–17; Daisy-Daisy/iStock, 18–19; monkeybusinessimages/iStock, 20–21.

Printed in the United States of America at Corporate Graphics in North Mankato, Minnesota.

GOALS AND TOOLS